HOW TO BE

~~GOOD~~

GREAT

AT YOUR JOB

HOW TO BE

~~GOOD~~

GREAT

AT YOUR JOB

Get things done. Get the credit. Get ahead.

JUSTIN KERR

CHRONICLE BOOKS
SAN FRANCISCO

Library of Congress Cataloging-in-Publication Data available.

ISBN 978-1-4521-6913-2

Manufactured in China

Design by Spencer Vandergrift

10 9 8 7 6 5 4 3 2 1

Chronicle books and gifts are available at special quantity discounts to corporations, professional associations, literacy programs, and other organizations. For details and discount information, please contact our premiums department at corporatesales@chroniclebooks.com or at 1-800-759-0190.

Chronicle Books LLC
680 Second Street
San Francisco, California 94107
www.chroniclebooks.com

Dedicated to Chris Funk.

My first boss. My best boss.

Contents:

8 / Introduction

10 / The basics

14/ Be accurate
17/ Be early

24 / How to work with other human beings

28/ Overcommunicate
32/ Make it easy to say yes
34/ If someone at work hates you

38 / How to give a presentation

42/ The perfect structure
46/ The perfect content

52 / How to write an email

57/ Six requirements of an awesome email

64/ How to win an email fight

68 / How to get promoted

72/ Setting your goals

77/ Understanding the playing field

83/ Making your case

90 / How to balance life and work

95/ How to create "me" time (during the workweek)

99/ How to leave work at work

101/ How to take time off

INTRODUCTION://

BEING GOOD AT YOUR JOB IS EASIER THAN YOU THINK.

People tend to get distracted by the politics of the workplace (bad bosses, unfair deadlines, conflicting priorities), but that's just noise, and none of it matters when it comes to finding your own personal success at work.

If you want to get promoted, leave work early, win an email fight, or make someone at work stop hating you, the formula is the same: take responsibility and overcommunicate like crazy.

I've worked at some of the biggest companies in the world, running billion-dollar businesses with hundreds of people reporting to me, and yet I've rarely worked past 5:00 p.m. or checked my email on the weekend. I call myself an efficiency monster, because I am obsessed with finding the easiest and cleanest way to do things.

Most people never realize that the reason they are working late is because they are losing two hours of their day waiting for people to reply to their (sucky) emails. Write better emails, leave work early, have a better life. Sometimes it really is that simple.

Whether you are new to the workforce or a veteran of middle management, your ability to get promoted and do awesome work ultimately hinges on whether you can do the little things right time and time again.

Let's get to work.

1.

The basics

IF YOU WANT TO BE GOOD AT YOUR JOB THERE ARE TWO FUNDAMENTAL BEHAVIORS TO WHICH YOU MUST ABSOLUTELY COMMIT YOURSELF:

Be early. Be accurate. Everything else will take care of itself.

More important than convincing people you're smart is convincing people they can trust you. Trust you to be on time. Trust you to deliver accurate information. Trust you to do what you say you are going to do.

Every time you turn in a report with a missing number, an incorrect formula, or a misspelled word you are saying, "I don't care enough." Every time you miss a deadline (even by fifteen minutes) you are saying, "You can't trust me." It sounds harsh, but small mistakes can have a cumulative effect on your reputation and your ability to get promoted.

Projects come and go. Office politics ebb and flow. But building a reputation as someone who delivers complete information in a timely manner (early) is the secret to long-term, sustainable success in the workplace.

Being accurate and being early—that is all that matters, so keep it simple: Do good work. Turn it in on time or ahead of time, if you can. Repeat.

BE ACCURATE

Being accurate is more important than being early, because if people don't believe what you're saying they won't care when, where, or how you say it. Simply put, being accurate is the foundation of your reputation at work.

It is far better to be a bit slower—and more accurate—than a bit faster and wrong. Understand this. Live this.

Being accurate is about more than just having the right number on an Excel spreadsheet. It is about delivering the right information at the right time in the right format.

In my experience there are two behaviors that can help you ensure accuracy: **breathing and asking questions.**

Take a deep breath

It is easy to get caught up in the hullabaloo of the workplace and convince yourself that hitting SEND on an email right now—instead of thirty seconds from now—is really, really important when, in fact, the exact opposite is true.

It is really, really unimportant whether you send that email now versus thirty seconds (or even two minutes) from now.

Haste makes waste, so my simple prescription for ensuring accuracy in your work on a consistent basis is to take a deep breath before you hit SEND. I literally want you to breathe slowly, in and out, every single time before you hit SEND. The goal is to create a trigger (a cue) to remind you to slow down and double-check your work before hitting SEND.

Make sure that the attachment is actually attached. Make sure the formulas all add up. Make sure the document is formatted to print on one page—not thirty-seven pages with one sentence on each. Make sure the day of the week and the date of the month match.

Of course, mistakes are going to happen, but you can at least eliminate the dumb ones.

Create your own mental checklist of things that could go wrong, and don't let them go wrong. Every detail matters, so take the extra thirty seconds, breathe, and check your work carefully.

If you make small mistakes on a regular basis (more than once per week), it doesn't matter how smart you (think you) are, people won't like working with you.

Pro Tip:

The same rules apply when someone asks you a question in a meeting.

Rather than being overanxious to always have an answer on the spot, take a deep breath and think before you speak. Trust me—no one will notice this split-second of breath (while you collect your thoughts), but people will notice if you tell a half-truth or your answer is jumbled and confusing. In fact, it is far better to admit you don't know the answer and instead offer to follow up within twenty-four hours, rather than fake it.

Ask clarifying questions

If someone asks you to do something, make sure you are 100 percent clear on what it is they actually want. Accepting vague direction from a boss, or anyone in the workplace, can be as dangerous to your reputation as your own laziness.

If something isn't clear, ask questions until you have all the information you need to proceed. This includes clarifying formats, file locations, timing, etc. . . .

Your ability to deliver good work is wholly dependent on your ability to get good inputs and clear directions. An extra thirty seconds of questions can often translate into hours of saved time (for you and your boss) by avoiding frustrating misunderstandings that result in extra work.

If someone asks you to complete a project by EOD (end of day), clarify if they mean 5:00 p.m., 6:00 p.m., or just before 9:00 a.m. the following day. This will help you avoid the situation of believing you have more time to work on a project, when your boss actually wanted it by 5:00 p.m.

Simply put: if you don't understand something, ask questions until you do.

BE EARLY

Ninety-two percent of your problems at work will go away if you show up to work earlier than you did yesterday. How early depends on your particular situation, but make no mistake: the secret to work-life balance, good relationships with your coworkers, and early promotions all rests on your ability to get to work early and turn in your work early. (Oh, and don't forget to leave work early—seriously—leave work early.)

Get to work early

If you want to be amazing at your job, get to work one hour early. Showing up to work at the same time as everyone else is a ticket to mediocrity—and a slow promotion.

One hour of work in peace and quiet is worth two hours in the office when other people are there, meetings are happening, and you're distracted.

Here's what you can accomplish in one extra hour:

- Read and reply to all emails that are outstanding
- Review your calendar and prepare for how the day will go
- Have time for any last-minute prep
- Review your to-do list
- Send out emails reminding people what you need from them
- Read your favorite website undisturbed

There's another upshot to getting to work early that's less tangible but just as important: you begin to build the perception that you are a top performer.

Look around at the other people that show up early. I bet you they are the most successful people in the company. This means something. It also means something if these people are seeing you at work early. As LeBron James once tweeted: "Game recognizes game."

Turn in your work early

Always aim to deliver your work twenty-four hours in advance of a deadline.

If your boss asks for something by EOD Thursday, you should send it to them by 5:00 p.m. on Wednesday. Why 5:00 p.m.? Because you want to get credit for delivering the work early, and it's much more impressive to deliver something the day before, rather than the morning of. By sending the document at 5:00 p.m., you are almost guaranteed to catch your boss before they go home for the day.

Think of your performance this way:

> **A** = Twenty-four hours in advance
>
> **B** = Same day as deadline
>
> **C** = At the deadline (5:00 p.m. on an EOD deadline)
>
> **D** = EOD on an EOD deadline (after 7:00 p.m.)
>
> **F** = Missed the deadline and gave no warning

Getting a C doesn't mean you're going to get fired, but it certainly won't be moving you ahead in the ranks.

And when it comes to those situations when you can't turn in your report twenty-four hours in advance, I recommend that you still send an email to your boss by 5:00 p.m. the day prior, giving them the status update and reassuring them of your progress: "I'm working on it. I just need to finalize a few details—but I will send to you by X-hour tomorrow."

Your goal is to control the flow of communication and stay ahead of your boss's concerns.

If your boss has to send an email asking about the project, you should interpret this as a signal that they are feeling anxious and you have missed an opportunity to update them.

● ● ●

Leave work early

Don't make the mistake of believing that if you work late people will think you're a hard worker.

If you work late, people will think you're behind, you can't keep up, you're overwhelmed, you don't have a life, you're late on a project—in short, you're not good at your job.

Get your work done. Ask if your boss needs anything else from you. Leave (early).

"Early" is a relative term, and EOD means something different to every person in the office, so my point is less about trying to race out of the office at 4:59 p.m. every day and more about feeling confident that leaving before other people in the office, far from being a problem, in fact highlights how good you are at your job. You're taking care of business.

This isn't something you need to ask permission to do; simply start doing it.

As Oprah Winfrey wisely said: "You teach people how you want to be treated" and when it comes to leaving work, the same rules apply: if you build a reputation as someone who leaves work at 6:00 p.m. every day, people will adjust their expectations and requests accordingly.

There is no right or wrong answer for the exact hour and minute that you leave work every day, so do what feels natural. If you aren't happy with your current situation (i.e., departure time), change it by employing the simple rule that for every thirty minutes earlier you get to work in the morning, you can leave one hour earlier at the end of the day, due to increased efficiency in the early-morning hours.

As Oprah Winfrey wisely said: "You teach people how you want to be treated" and when it comes to leaving work, the same rules apply: if you build a reputation as someone who leaves work at 6:00 p.m. every day, people will adjust their expectations and requests accordingly.

BONUS: MEET WEEKLY

If you don't meet with your boss on a weekly basis, you are going to have a hard time being successful at your job. This meeting should be a dedicated thirty-minute block that is regularly scheduled every week. If it isn't happening, ask for it. In fact, demand it (politely, of course).

The purpose of this meeting is to stay on the same page as your boss by sharing timely updates, getting approvals, and resolving open issues. This is your meeting. You should schedule it. You should set the agenda. And you should lead it.

Don't leave anything to chance, because without this meeting it will be impossible for you to manage expectations and get credit for all the work you do. In fact, if you don't have this meeting, you are conceding control of your career to your boss— and we both know that the chances you have a good boss are less than 50/50—so don't screw this up.

There are three steps to creating a successful weekly meeting:

- **GET THE TIMING RIGHT:**
  Don't schedule on a Monday— there are too many things happening on a Monday. And don't schedule on a Friday—no one likes meetings on a Friday. You want to aim for early morning if possible, because if the meeting is scheduled for late afternoon on a Tuesday, there's a high likelihood that other meetings will take priority or your boss will run late and you'll lose your scheduled time. If your meeting time keeps getting moved, identify and recommend a better time that can become consistent.

- **SEND AN AGENDA:**
  Email your boss a bullet-point list of topics by 5:00 p.m. the day prior to your weekly meeting. Doing so ensures that the meeting is not cancelled, helps you organize your own thoughts, and gives your boss a heads up in case they need to prepare for a certain topic or decision. Sending an agenda says, "I'm awesome. I'm organized. I'm good at my job."

- **LEAD THE MEETING:**
  It is critical that you go into the meeting with the mind frame that it's your meeting to run. You set the agenda, you lead the discussion, you ask the questions, you get the answers. Come prepared with specific questions. What exactly do you need an answer on? Have all the facts ready so your boss can make a decision on the spot. Your job is to make it easy for them to say yes.

Done correctly, this weekly 1:1 meeting can put you on the promotion superhighway. Vroom. Vroom.

2.

How to work with other human beings

LIKE IT OR NOT, HAVING A JOB USUALLY REQUIRES THAT YOU INTERACT WITH OTHER PEOPLE.

Whether it is a frustrating coworker, an overachieving peer, or a rah-rah boss, it is important to acknowledge that everyone is human. We have good days and bad days. We have sick kids at home, hangovers, rent that is due, and a vacation that needs to be booked.

This fundamental reality is often overlooked within all the rituals and hierarchies of the workplace. It is important that you don't fall into the trap of treating people like robots who exist only to take or give orders.

Human beings are incredibly complicated, moody, emotional, unreliable, strange, and wondrous creatures, so my advice for working with other people is simple: overcommunicate, make it easy for other people to say yes, and if someone at work hates you, address the situation directly.

OVERCOMMUNICATE

The most common complaint that I hear from people in the workplace is "I don't get credit for all the work I do." Inherent in this frustration is an unrealistic expectation that your boss is a mind reader.

Just because you did something (filled out a report, replied to an email, spent three hours preparing for the presentation) doesn't mean that everyone else knows about it.

It is your responsibility to tell people (especially your boss) what you are doing, as well as when and how you are going to do it. Your goal should be to try and get credit for a project at least three times (beginning, middle, end), rather than once (only when you turn it in).

The simple truth is that it isn't enough to do the work.

It's everything that happens before and during the project that ultimately influences people's perception of your ability to get things done.

Communication goes two ways—inbound and outbound. Your goal should be to increase your outbound communication (updates, progress reports, agendas) as much as possible in order to limit (and head off) inbound questions and concerns. The more you tell people what you are doing (outbound), the less they will try and tell you what you need to do (inbound).

Let's look at this more closely.

The problem

Here is what people think happens on a project:

1. Your boss asks you to do something
2. You go away and do it
3. You present it back to your boss

Here is what actually happens on a project:

1. Your boss asks you to do something
2. You go away and work on it
3. Your boss asks you if you are working on the project
4. You say you are working on it
5. A few hours (or days) later your boss asks again if you are going to be ready for the deadline
6. You say yes
7. You present the project to your boss

The key point is that most people don't consider the importance of their boss's experience during the journey to complete a project.

Most people are so focused on themselves and their own experience—"I finished the project on time, so what's the problem?"—that they completely miss the fact that their boss was left in the dark with no visibility to progress along the way.

Think of it this way: each time your boss asks you if you are working on the project, what they are really saying is: "I'm feeling anxious because I haven't heard from you, and I'm worried that the work won't get done."

Because the project required multiple inquiries from your boss, they may walk away from the experience feeling that it was their follow-ups that ensured the project was delivered on time. This leads to a situation where your boss may walk away from the project and feel like they did all the work—not you.

This is the crux of the "I don't get credit for all the work I do" complaint.

You very well may have been on top of every aspect of the project, but the fact that your boss asked you—instead of you telling them—that's the difference between getting credit for a project (and building trust) versus getting no credit and being perceived as unreliable.

How to fix the problem

I call this the "get credit four times instead of one time" approach, a.k.a. "my boss loves me and I get promoted all the time" approach.

1. Your boss asks you to do something

2. You send your boss a quick email by EOD with an outline of how you will accomplish the project and the key (specific) timelines you will work toward, including check-in points

3. You work on the project

4. You give your boss an update during your weekly 1:1 meetings or you send a quick status email saying everything is on schedule. Keep reminding them of the timeline you had agreed to earlier. It's usually best just to forward that original email with a quick comment.

5. You send an email by 5:00 p.m. the day before the project is due with a simple title and message: Pre-Read: Project X. "Hey Boss, I wanted to send you a copy of the final project in advance of tomorrow's deadline. If you have any questions or comments I'm happy to adjust before the meeting tomorrow."

6. You turn in the project (at the meeting), etc. . . . .

There is no magic here. It's just a matter of taking a few minutes to give your boss an update every now and then.

Don't overthink it by being worried that a small update is meaningless or a waste of your boss's "precious" time. Trust me, your boss would far prefer getting too many updates versus chasing you around like a babysitter trying to find out what you are up to.

Don't worry about asking for permission to send updates—just start doing it. If it ever becomes too much, they will tell you. (In my seventeen years of corporate experience I've never had a boss ask me to keep them in the dark or share less information with them, so I wouldn't be too worried about this happening.)

Pro Tip:

Forwarding emails to your boss is a really easy way to share updates with minimal effort.

You don't have to write an essay. Just a simple heads up should suffice: "Hey Boss, just a quick FYI . . . below is an update from Casey on the budget proposal that is due later this week. Everything is on track. Let me know if you have any questions." Whether your boss reads the email or not, their experience of you is that you communicate effectively and provide updates in a timely manner. This engenders trust as well as recognition of all the work you do. #winning

---

MAKE IT EASY
TO SAY YES

When it comes to getting approvals, it is your responsibility to make it easy for the other person to say yes. Whether you want approval for a $1 million budget or approval of your vacation time, the key is to start small and be specific, while also anticipating people's concerns.

I want to use a simple example to make my point:

If you want to ask someone to be your mentor you don't start by walking up to them and saying, "Hi, I was hoping you would be my mentor for the next three years and we could spend a lot of time together and I could ask you a lot of questions and hopefully you can help me get promoted because other people will be impressed that you are my mentor."

This is exactly the wrong approach because you haven't made it easy for the other person to say yes. You've asked for too much too soon, and as a result, you've made an unreasonably intimidating proposal.

Try this instead:

"Hi, my name is Justin Kerr. I really admire what you've accomplished at this company, in particular the way that you turned around the kids' business, and I was hoping that I could steal fifteen minutes of your time, buy you a coffee, and ask you a few questions? If it works for you I could follow up with your assistant to find some time in the next three to four weeks."

Do you see what I did there? There were three key elements of my approach:

- **Start small:** I only asked for fifteen minutes. Everyone has fifteen minutes. Sure, you may want more time than fifteen minutes, but your first goal is to get a "yes" (however small) and build from there. Take your big request and break it into bite-size chunks that are more easily swallowed.

- **Be specific AND flexible:** When trying to get to yes, it is important for you to understand what is essential and what is flexible. In this case, it doesn't matter if I get coffee with the person this week or four weeks from now, so I combined my specific minimal request (fifteen minutes) with a big window of opportunity (three to four weeks), thus increasing the likelihood that the person can't say no—thus leading to a yes.

- **Flattery will get you everywhere:** Everyone is human, and as such, everyone likes to hear they're doing a good job. Even the CEO wants someone to slap them on the back and say, "Great presentation!"— so why not you? (Hint: The more specific your compliment, the more genuine it will feel.)

Getting to yes is a skill. If you get rejected, don't get mad. Sit down, put yourself in the other person's shoes, and figure out where you went wrong.

Pro Tip:
Last-minute requests are a no-no.

No one likes to be put in a situation of having to make a decision under pressure (or with a lot of people watching). Do everything you can to stay ahead of deadlines, because the more time you can give your boss to consider the idea without outside pressures, the more likely you can resolve any concerns and get to yes. Remember: surprises are your enemy, so don't surprise your boss with a last-minute request.

IF SOMEONE AT WORK HATES YOU

It is inevitable that at some point in your career you are going to come across someone who just straight up doesn't like you.

Sometimes you'll know why the person hates you, and sometimes it will be a total mystery, but no matter whether it's personal, professional, or political, the process of making someone stop disliking you is the same.

You need to figure out why they hate you, and then discuss it with them directly.

Step 1: Figure out why they hate you

People don't hate people for no reason. Whether big or small, there is always something.

Start by asking yourself: "Did I do something to really piss this person off? Did I do something that would justify them not liking me? Is there anything (and I mean anything) I could have done to contribute to this situation?" Even if it was unintentional or taken in the wrong way, it's good to know where it started.

Once you've performed an honest self-assessment, you are ready to seek insights from trusted people around you. This is a delicate situation. There is a right way and a wrong way to talk to other people about someone who dislikes you. Let's start with the wrong way.

The wrong approach is to shout it from the rooftops or try and wage a negative campaign against the person who dislikes you. This will only heighten the tension rather than resolve it. It is important to recognize that nobody "wins" these inner-office Hunger Games. The workplace is not a kill-or-be-killed scenario, and if you come across a coworker who seems determined to work against you, don't waste energy trying to throw the other person under the bus or paint them in a negative light.

Here's the right way: Talk with your fellow coworkers, boss, or HR in a simple and open-ended manner:

"Hey, I'm hoping to get your advice. Person X doesn't seem to like me and I can't quite figure out why. I want to fix the relationship so we can continue to work well together. Do you have any insights for me or advice on working with them?"

Your goal is to shine a light on the problem while also claiming the higher moral ground.

Maybe everyone else doesn't realize that the person has it out for you. Maybe the crowd experiences each criticism or each comment that this person makes toward you as a simple counterpoint. Maybe they don't see what's going on.

By making everyone aware that you feel this person doesn't like you, you are successfully reframing the way everyone else (coworkers, bosses, HR) will view the person's next criticism toward you. The next time they hear a sharp remark, they're going to see it in light of your attempts to make peace.

By seeking advice in a quiet manner from the people around you, you frame the debate in your favor and make yourself the sympathetic party. Nina Simone's lyrics feel particularly relevant: "I'm just a girl whose intentions are good. Oh Lord, please don't let me be misunderstood."

Step 2: Talk to the person
(who hates you)

In order to resolve the conflict, you must speak directly to the person who doesn't like you. This is the moment of truth and, as much as you were hoping that I was going to tell you that you didn't have to talk to the person, this issue won't resolve itself if you don't address it directly.

The key is to keep it simple and use their humanity to your advantage.

- **Ask for five minutes:** If you ask for thirty minutes, they are likely to say they are too busy, so just get your foot in the door by asking for five minutes.

- **Own it:** The first thing you want to do is take responsibility—you need to quickly establish that you aren't here to complain (or blame). Instead you are here to resolve whatever is wrong. This will emotionally disarm your opponent and you will likely discover a decent human being sitting in front of you. By humbling yourself first, you make it acceptable (and likely) for them to match your behavior.

- **Ask what you can do to improve the relationship:** Try something as simple as "It seems like we aren't connecting in the way that I'd like to, is there something that I've done to upset you? I was thinking it might have something to do with my comment last week in the meeting when I said X."

- **Shut up and listen:** After you've demonstrated a willingness to take responsibility for the situation, let them talk. Maybe it had nothing to do with the meeting last week, but by offering up a specific example you have actually opened the door for them to tell you what is bothering them.

Maybe there isn't a problem. Maybe there is no issue at all and you've invented this entire scenario in your head. Maybe the other person didn't realize that what they were doing was actually causing you concern. In any of these cases, the other person (hopefully) will take some responsibility for the misunderstanding and you can both feel more connected (and careful) as a result of this conversation.

If you get hit with a full-frontal denial: "I have no idea what you are talking about," then it is best to end the meeting as quickly as possible (while still being polite), because nothing you say or do will be able help. Even if the other person doesn't meet you halfway, you've won the day, because bullies don't like to be confronted in a nonconfrontational manner.

In my experience with such matters, nine times out of ten you can resolve the situation and move forward amicably. It doesn't mean that you are going to be best friends (although sometimes that does happen), but at least you won't live your life worrying about someone or something that constantly bothers you.

No matter what the outcome, you've done the right thing. Congratulations.

Pro Tip:

Make sure you circle back.

Go chat with every single person you spoke to during the buildup to the actual meeting (with your hater). If everything was resolved, it is important to close the loop so everyone sees that you are a person who can solve problems effectively. This is a critical step, because you want to control the narrative and protect yourself against any future bad-mouthing (especially in the case of someone who wants no part of resolving the tension).

3.

How to give a presentation

CONTRARY TO POPULAR BELIEF, THE WORLD IS NOT SPLIT INTO GOOD PRESENTERS AND BAD PRESENTERS.

The world is split into people who take extra time to organize their thoughts and people who ramble. Whether you are a CEO or an entry-level assistant, your goal with any presentation is high impact AND high recall for your audience.

There are two important aspects of giving a good presentation: structure and content. If you have one without the other, you will fail. (So read this entire chapter.)

THE PERFECT
STRUCTURE

If you create a simple framework for your message and repeat yourself as often as possible, you can become a strong communicator.

The good news is that once you master this structure you can use it for every presentation you give for the rest of your life, no matter the audience, the setting, or topic.

It's just six simple steps:

- The one-sentence overview
- Explain the structure
- Give them the headlines
- Present each topic
- Tell them what's next
- The one-sentence conclusion

Here is a sample presentation based on this structure.

Step 1: The one-sentence overview

Tell them what you're going to tell them.

"I am here to present the Boys' Winter Outerwear Collection."

Step 2: Explain the structure

Let your audience know exactly how many points they should listen for.

"There are three main points I want to discuss."

Enumerating is an important detail, because it helps them structure their note-taking, so be sure to say a number. You are saying, "I am organized— therefore, listen up."

Step 3: Give them the headlines

Announce the big headlines you're going to talk about.

"I want to talk about nylon fabrication, length, and price points."

You never want people to struggle to follow what you're saying or have to search for your key facts. When you give your audience clear headlines, you are practically writing their notes for them and increasing the chances that they will pay attention to what you are saying, as well as remember what you said. This is a good thing.

Step 4: Present each topic

You're now ready to present your first topic. Cue your audience that you're starting a topic. Then cover the topic. Then summarize what you just covered.

"The first thing I want to talk about is nylon fabrication. Nylon fabrication is the biggest trend in the market and I see an opportunity for us to . . . OK, so that's why I think nylon fabrication is going to be really important for us next season."

Every topic you cover should follow the same pattern: cue, present, summarize.

The repetition at the beginning and end of each topic might seem unnecessary, but your audience will appreciate these organizing cues.

Step 5: Tell them what's next

You want to keep reinforcing your structure throughout and direct people as you move from one topic to another. Not only does this help reengage a wandering listener, it also builds a sense of momentum in your presentation. Two down, one to go.

"OK, we've talked about length, so now I want to talk about price points. I think we have five minutes left for this last topic."

Don't overlook the importance of letting people know how much longer the presentation is going to be. This helps people relax. They don't have to worry about time and can focus instead on what you're saying.

Think of all the times you've listened to someone and thought, "OH MY GOSH—how long is this person going to talk?" Your only recourse is to guess how many pages of notes they have left in their hands. People who are worried about how much longer you're going to talk are not paying attention to a single word you're saying. Give the people what they want— let them know how much more of their time you are taking.

Step 6: The one-sentence conclusion

Remind your audience of what you've told them. It should only be one sentence.

"OK, so we have talked about nylon fabrication, why we're going to add longer-length jackets, and opportunities to raise price points—does anyone have any questions?"

Open the floor for questions. You're done.

Pro Tip:

Skip the handouts.

When it comes to handouts during the presentation, I usually advise against them unless you have a very number-intensive presentation. The minute you give people something to look at, you no longer control their attention—or the flow of information.

If you must use handouts, it is essential that they are organized and easy to follow. Making sure that your words, actions, and handouts all say the same thing (in the same order) creates a powerful harmony in the listener's experience of your presentation.

THE PERFECT
CONTENT

The content of a presentation can be boiled down to two elements: what is happening and what are you going to do about it. Hero facts and action steps.

Hero facts

One of the things you'll quickly discover in the business world is that there's so much data available that you have nearly unlimited numbers to support your argument—so which do you choose?

Should you use percentages, average weekly sales, total monthly sales, sell-through percentages, gross margin? It's easy to make a laundry list of numbers and throw them at someone—but no one likes that. And more important, no one remembers that.

If your goal is to get people's attention and inspire action, it is important that you fill your presentation with hero facts. A hero fact is a singular point of evidence that stands out in a crowd. It is the "sound bite" that is easily digestible, and thus easy to remember. It isn't a single number or a single fact that matters—it's the way you construct them and the story you tell that takes them from simple facts to hero facts.

Building a hero fact is a three-step process:

- **Find the number:** I recommend asking yourself the following: "If I could only use one number to prove my point, what would it be?" My quick rule of thumb is that if you can't memorize the number, then it's probably too complicated—and you shouldn't use it. At its most basic level, this challenges you to think: Should you say 265,321 units or should you say 265,000 units? Or, depending on the context of the number in the bigger picture, should you say about 300,000 units?

- **Set the context:** Equally important to picking the right number is setting the context in which that number exists. If I tell you that I hit fifty-two home runs in high school, it could sound like a lot or not many, depending on the context in which I give it. If I tell you that I hit fifty-two home runs my senior year, which was a state record, that is impressive. If I tell you I hit fifty-two home runs over my four-year career, including on my junior varsity team . . . less impressive.

- **Make it surprising:** With so many numbers being exchanged in any given meeting, it is always a good idea to try to make your hero fact stand out in a crowd. An effective way to do this is to make a connection between your fact and a surprising detail—the more specific the better. For example: Rather than telling your boss that if you change the weight of the fabric from 3 grams to 2.6 grams, you can decrease the cost of production by $0.25, it would be far more compelling to explain that you can decrease costs by 20 percent ($0.25) if you decrease the weight of the fabric 0.4 grams, which is the equivalent of the weight of a single piece of tissue paper. (Creating a mental picture of tissue paper makes this tangible, easy to remember, and easy to say yes to, because the analogy you created minimizes the decision to feel less risky.)

Creating hero facts takes time and effort, so most people don't bother to do it, but if you take the extra step to create compelling content, your audience is more likely to pay attention—and your boss is more likely to trust you in front of senior management. Up, up, and away.

● ● ●

Action steps

The definition of an action step is a concrete movement you take toward achieving a goal or solving a problem. By definition, it is specific, measurable, and almost always associated with a deadline: "X is happening, so I will do Y (by Z time)."

Don't present an idea and leave it for others to interpret or wonder what the point is. You always want to lead the discussion, and by recommending your action step(s), you give meaning to the facts and figures.

If something is going wrong, don't just say it's going wrong—say what you're going to do about it. If something is going well, don't just brag about it—tell me how you are going to maximize the opportunity and what comes next.

This is also the appropriate time to call out whether you need other people's support, approval, or involvement to keep proceeding. The action step is the output of your presentation. It is your answer to the ever-present question "So what?"

If something is going wrong, don't just say it's going wrong— say what you're going to do about it. If something is going well, don't just brag about it— tell me how you are going to maximize the opportunity and what comes next.

BONUS: PRACTICE MAKES PERFECT

Practice. Practice. Practice.

If you want to be a good presenter, you have to practice. Unfortunately, the workplace is not necessarily conducive to getting a lot of reps in low-pressure situations, because everyone is so busy just trying to keep their nose above water and complete today's or tomorrow's project/deadline.

In a normal business setting, you might get to make a presentation to your colleagues once a week. After that, the frequency of presenting to a group becomes more sporadic and dependent on your title and job responsibilities. If you're entry-level, it may even be nonexistent—in which case, you may spend the first year of your work life making no progress toward improving an essential skill (presenting).

To fix this, here's what I recommend you do: find a friend or colleague, and in the absence of either of these, find an administrative assistant. Ask them if you can have fifteen minutes of their time once a week, and stand in front of them and give a presentation. (Schedule it as a recurring meeting every week, or it likely won't happen.)

The physical act of standing is important, because you will feel more exposed, which heightens all your senses—good and bad. It doesn't matter what the topic is—it only matters that you are standing in front of someone and speaking words out of your mouth. For bonus points, encourage your listener to ask at least one question with each practice presentation.

By making practice a priority and following this simple approach, you can instantly double, triple, or even quadruple the number of presentations you give in a year. If you finish the year having given fifty-two more presentations than your peers, even if they are "fake" presentations, advantage: you.

If you finish the year having given fifty-two more presentations than your peers, even if they are "fake" presentations, advantage: you.

4.

How to write an email

EMAIL IS THE SINGLE MOST IMPORTANT MEANS OF COMMUNICATION IN CORPORATE AMERICA. PERIOD.

Presentations are good and all, but if you think you are going to change people's opinions or get a key decision made by being a passionate and articulate presenter, you will quickly become frustrated (and ineffective), because presentations are a relatively tiny part of your job—especially when compared to the amount of information transfer that takes place day to day and hour by hour through email.

With email, you don't have to wait for someone else to schedule it or approve it; you can do it anytime you want (and as often as you want). This is good and bad.

Most people don't stop to think: *Is this a good email? Is this information being presented in such a manner that it will solicit the reply I am looking for? Have I made it easy for the recipient to take action (without five more clarifying emails back and forth)? How am I using the subject line to draw the recipient's attention?*

It's a shame, because so much value (and time) is lost through ineffective emails. Teams and entire organizations waste thousands of hours per week—asking follow-up questions, waiting for follow-up answers to the follow-up questions, and asking follow-up questions to the follow-up answers to the original follow-up question.

If you aren't sure if you write good emails, here is the best way to check:

Pull up your inbox and scan it for the number of replies to a single email. It probably started simply enough. You wanted to tell everyone that their recap was due by Friday. But then you didn't attach the format, so someone had to ask you how to submit the information. Someone else wasn't clear if it was due Friday or EOD Friday. Someone else wasn't sure how they should even find the information to recap. All of a sudden your original email has a bunch of replies over two days and no actual work has even been accomplished.

I'm here to help.

● ● ●

SIX REQUIREMENTS OF AN AWESOME EMAIL

The rules of good communication are roughly the same whether you're standing in front of a hundred people, talking one-on-one with your boss, or using this crazy thing called email.

But one important point of distinction when it comes to email is the fact that your message is going to be competing with potentially hundreds of other emails to get the recipient's attention and (hopefully) engagement.

Most people don't stop to think: What is the recipient's experience of this email going to be? Will they read it on a desktop computer or, more likely, a tiny iPhone screen? Will they be running between meetings with only thirty seconds to scan their inbox for the most pressing (or interesting) subject?

Just as people tend to blame their boss for "not giving them credit for all the work they do" (see page 28), so too people blame their boss (or coworker) for not replying to their emails quickly enough, when in fact the real blame most likely is with the sender.

Was the email easy to read? Did the subject line communicate the urgency of the request? Was the information in this email organized in such a way as to allow the recipient to easily decipher what was needed from them? At its most basic level, was this a good email?

Writing good emails can have a defining impact on your career AND your personal life.

It can be the difference between working until 8:00 p.m. every day or leaving work at 5:30 p.m. because you got all the replies you needed and could finish your work in a timely manner.

Here are the six requirements of an awesome email:

- Subject
- Deadlines
- Bullet points
- Jump to conclusions
- White space
- The attachment trap

Subject

Make sure your subject line is specific, punchy, and action-oriented: Q2 Project: Action Required: Chris Goble + Mauri Skinfill

This is the first thing that people see, so it is your most important call to action. Don't bury the lede and subtly request Chris's help to complete your project at the end of the email. Put it in the subject line so that you have Chris's attention and he realizes there is something you need from him before he even opens the email.

Equally important to being specific is the need to be succinct.

The fewer words the better, so rewrite your subject heading a few times until you are satisfied that it captures the essential purpose of the information you need to communicate in as few words as possible.

The subject line of an email is a make-or-break moment for you. If it fails to grab the recipient's attention (as they are running between meetings), it is likely to be skipped over and opened later in the day when they have "more time to catch up." Bummer, now you can't get your work done and you have to work late. Sucks to be you.

Deadlines

If there is a deadline in your email, meaning you need someone to do something by a specific time, you must include it in the subject line: Budget Overview: Due Tuesday, 3:36 p.m.

It is your responsibility to ensure that what you need to happen by what time is clearly legible for the recipient at first glance. This means that it needs to stand out from everything else in the email. Use **bold**, highlight it in red, etc. . . .

Be sure to make the deadline as clear as possible, so use as much detail as you can. The worst mistake you can make when setting a deadline is using EOD (end of day).

EOD is also the white noise of corporate speak. Think about when you walk down the hall and someone asks you, "How's it going?" and before you have time to even stop and turn around to answer their question, they've simply walked right past you. EOD is the same thing. It is ubiquitous, and therefore useless.

One trick I like to use is setting a deadline with an offbeat time—Due 4:47 p.m. Wednesday. By choosing an unusual time for the deadline, you increase the likelihood of your recipient paying attention. After all, it's way more eye-catching to see a deadline for 4:47 p.m. on Wednesday versus the generic EOD.

Pro Tip:

When you get into work early in the morning, check your email for any outstanding deadlines due that day.

If you see any, forward your original email to the recipients with a simple message: "Hi John, just wanted to make sure we were on track for the deadline today at 2 p.m.? Let me know if any questions/concerns." Re-upping your deadline is a great way to ensure that John will prioritize your email.

Bullet points

If I was ever forced to boil my entire work life into a single suggestion, it would be this: use bullet points.

Bullet points project, "I am organized—therefore, pay attention to what I am telling you." This is a good thing.

Don't use a dash (-), asterisk (*), underscore (_), or indent to organize your information, because, depending on the make and model of each recipient's machine, these informal formatting tools may look completely different (and unorganized) on each person's screen. Bullet points are presented exactly the same way on every single device, big and small, Mac or tablet, phone or desktop.

When using bullet points, you should limit yourself to only one sentence per bullet. If you are using more than one sentence per bullet, you are either rambling or making more than one point.

Jump to conclusions

Get right to the point in your emails. Remember that your recipient reads a lot of emails every day, so don't waste their time. The longer it takes to get to the point, the greater the chance that they will miss it. Just start with the conclusion or the big takeaway, and then put the rest of the information after that.

This isn't seventh grade. Your email doesn't need an introduction, supporting evidence, and a summary paragraph at the end. Flip that sh*t around and do exactly the opposite of what your middle school teacher taught you. Start with the conclusion, and then list supporting evidence.

I assume that if I write a strong enough subject line and first sentence (conclusion), then most people won't even bother to read the rest of my email. My goal is to make it easy for them to say yes and give me whatever it is I need from them.

Pro Tip:
Pay attention to what will be visible when people first open your email.

What can the reader see without having to scroll down? You have to get all your key points (conclusion, action steps, and deadlines) above the scroll, which means in the first three lines of an email, or people may miss your point.

White space

Designing an email is as important as the content itself. If the email isn't easy to read and well organized, people are much more likely to skip it until later—or miss the point you're trying to make altogether.

Most people don't give a moment's thought to the actual appearance of their email. Most people click REPLY and basically puke their thoughts onto the keyboard. Don't be one of these people.

The trick is to give the information room to breathe.

White space is your friend, so I recommend that you use the RETURN key liberally (at least twice between paragraphs and bullet points). This creates a visual break (white space) between each point and avoids the situation where bullet points get stacked together, creating the same visual intimidation as a block of text.

I encourage you to declutter your emails as much as possible, so my advice is to lose the "signature" flourishes and inspirational quotes at the bottom of your email.

It is your responsibility to make the email easy to read and attractive to look at. A simple rule of thumb is the fewer words, the better.

The attachment trap

I operate on an assumption that no one opens attachments and, therefore, I always provide a summary in the body of the email itself.

Especially in today's mobile world, opening attachments on tiny screens across separate operating platforms (Word versus Pages versus Google Docs versus Dropbox) can be such an inconvenience that your email is likely to be skipped until later in the day or ignored altogether.

Therefore, it is incumbent upon you to not rely on the attachment as a stand-alone document. Even in those cases when an attachment might be required, be sure to provide a succinct summary of key points or next steps in the body of the email, thus avoiding the most awful of email crimes— sending an email with no content (totally blank) and expecting the recipient to open the attachment and figure it out.

These email rules about attachments are all about showing respect for the recipient and putting their experience above your own small inconvenience of typing out a few lines to provide context for the attachment. Just as no man is an island (John Donne), so too should no attachment be an email unto itself.

Pro Tip:

If you do send an attachment, you better make sure it is formatted to print.

Not formatting a document to print is a super effective way to make everyone hate you.

HOW TO WIN AN
EMAIL FIGHT

If you ever find yourself in an email fight—and trust me you will—the only thing you have to remember to do is step away from the email. You cannot win an email fight over email.

No matter how much you don't like the person, no matter how wrong they are (and right you are), no matter how you got there, you have to step away from the computer and resolve it person to person.

Keep it simple. Get up from your desk, find the person, and have a discussion.

"Hey, can we talk about that email? It seems like we have a missed connection, and I wanted to resolve it in person. Do you have a minute?"

Then proceed to (softly) negotiate your differences. You'll be shocked at how quickly all of their (email) bluster fades away when they are actually face-to-face with another human being. You may even find that there was no real dispute at all, and the email medium was to blame for what seemed like an antagonistic tone.

If other people were involved in the email chain, make sure that immediately after you resolve the dispute you go back to your desk and send an email, cc'ing everyone, with a simple message that says something like,

"Hi Everyone, Josh and I were able to connect on this topic, and here is how we would like to proceed."

You've diffused a conflict with a colleague AND you've clearly demonstrated an ability to get things done. **You win.**

No matter how much you don't like the person, no matter how wrong they are (and right you are), no matter how you got there, you have to step away from the computer and resolve it person-to-person.

BONUS: WHAT'S BLACK AND WHITE AND READ ALL OVER?

Emails may seem transitory, but once you hit SEND they are as good as written in stone.

Emails can reach wide audiences, some of whom you may not have originally intended to read your message. Free of context, tone, and personal intimacy, emails can be manipulated, misunderstood, and potentially harmful.

If you write a bad email—use the wrong language, talk about something or someone in the wrong way—best of luck walking that back. The email can take on a life of its own, possibly ending up in the wrong person's inbox and landing you an invitation to HR.

On the flip side, if you are writing good emails and presenting yourself in an effective way, your message can travel to people within the organization to whom you wouldn't normally have access. Your email becomes your ambassador to the upper echelons of management.

So, take a step back and consider whether you are spending enough time making sure every email, like every presentation, represents you in an effective and positive manner.

If you write a bad email— use the wrong language, talk about something or someone in the wrong way—best of luck walking that back.

5.

How to get promoted

BETTER TITLE. BETTER OFFICE. BETTER PAY. MAKE DAD HAPPY.

We all have our reasons for wanting to get promoted, but most people don't know how to make it happen.

Sure, in some rare cases you'll be promoted at the exact moment when you really deserve it—but in reality, you're just as likely to be promoted for being in the right place at the right time. Likewise, you may get passed over because of circumstances out of your control, despite really deserving a promotion.

The purpose of this chapter is to change you from a passive participant in the process of your promotion into an active driver who is in charge of setting your goals, understanding the playing field, and making your case.

There are a lot of things that go into being promoted, which most people don't understand, but if you can focus on these three key elements you'll have a better chance than most.

SETTING YOUR GOALS

The first step to getting promoted is setting your goals. It sounds easy, but most people are so anxious to get promoted they see the goal-writing stage as a nuisance rather than a necessity.

Working toward a promotion without clear goals is like saying you are going to drive cross-country from San Francisco to New York City, but you don't have time to look up directions because you don't want to be late.

Remember what we said in Chapter One about the importance of accuracy versus speed (page 14)? It does you no good to try to move fast and accomplish something if that something isn't the right thing. Don't confuse action for progress when it comes to the promotion process.

To speed up your process of goal setting, here are four specific rules that will help you get promoted quickly:

- Be specific
- Write one-month goals
- Accomplish two big things
- Pick a day, any day

Be specific

Be very specific. There is a big difference between telling your boss, "I will work really hard," versus "I will beat projections by 25 percent, schedule and lead weekly cross-functional meetings, and work to improve store satisfaction by 10 percent."

Writing quantifiable goals is essential to moving the judgment of your performance from emotional to factual during your year-end review.

You aren't going to improve your financial skills—you are going to set a one-hour meeting every week with your financial planner to study your monthly forecast.

You aren't going to improve inter-office relationships—you are going to set weekly 1:1 meetings with all your key partners and solicit feedback from the team at three-, six-, and twelve-month periods to measure improvement.

You aren't going to beat projections—you are going to rate your performance down to specific percentages: A = 5 percent over projection; B = 0 to 4.9 percent over projection; C = anything under projection.

If you don't write specific goals, you put other people's feelings and emotions in charge of your promotion.

Feeling lucky?

If you write down specific goals, you don't have to rely on luck. You can let your results do the talking.

Write one-month goals

Goals with shorter time frames are easier to measure and therefore more useful in guiding or changing behavior. My favorite are one-month goals.

Writing your goals with an eye toward the year-end review is a mistake, because what you will end up with are broad, generic goals that won't be useful as guides to your day-to-day work and priorities.

If you set yourself a goal to master a new skill (or eliminate a weakness) every four weeks, you will have acquired twelve new skills by the end of the year. Compare this to the alternative of a bloated, generic, year-long blah-blah goal, and the benefits are obvious.

This process should never end throughout your entire career.

Make time every month to review your past month's goals and to set new goals for the coming month. There is always another skill for you to master, and by committing to a process of learning one new skill per month—no matter how small—you will quickly stockpile these small arms into a powerful arsenal. Multiply this by a few years, and wow—hello, Mr. President.

Pro Tip:

I also love three-month goals (and you should too).

Three months is the optimal length of time to measure a meaningful goal. While one-month goals may help your performance in the day-to-day workflow, three-month goals will be noticeable achievements that can directly help you get promoted. I like to call them flagship accomplishments. They should include major milestone achievements or new strategy initiatives that you identified, proposed, and produced.

Accomplish two big things

Simply doing your job is a good start, but it likely won't get you promoted—at least not in the time frame that you're hoping for. You need to undertake at least two flagship accomplishments in the next six months if you want to move from "could be promoted" to "front of the line for promotion."

This means you need to create and accomplish at least two high-visibility projects that everyone can agree went above and beyond your day-to-day normal responsibilities.

Examples could include leading a project across multiple teams, recommending a new business strategy for growth, or even something as simple as initiating after-work charity hours in your department.

Pick a day, any day

You need to get past any discomfort in bringing up the topic of promotion, because it is completely unrealistic to think you will be promoted if you and your boss have not talked about it consistently during the past year. You need to make sure your boss knows you want to be promoted—and when—so pick a date to aim for and talk about it with your boss.

Having this conversation early (at least nine months prior to your desired promotion) will ensure you both have the same perception of your current performance and potential for promotion.

Of course, your boss will probably never guarantee you a promotion on a certain day, but you should at least align on a general sense of timing—twelve months, eighteen months, etc.

Usually promotions are handed out at year-end or midyear, so use these already existing milestones as a starting place, and partner with your boss to get as specific as possible—hopefully to the month level.

Pro Tip:

There is an art and a science to talking about promotions.

It is important that you learn how to talk about wanting a promotion without making everyone hate you. The key is to frame your desire for promotion as wanting a chance to have a bigger impact on the business, take on more responsibility, have access to more meetings, learn new skills, and have new experiences.

Don't talk about your desire for a title as a motivating factor for your promotion, and don't compare yourself to weaker coworkers as a justification for your own promotion. (Comparing yourself to others will result in a long and unhappy life.) Don't bring up your desire for a promotion more than once a month. This can give the impression that all you care about is the promotion (me, me, me)—not the success of the business or the team (not a good look for someone trying to get promoted). Instead, frame the discussions around your goals and what you're working on.

UNDERSTANDING THE PLAYING FIELD

The second step in building your case for promotion is to know who the key decision makers are. Without understanding the landscape of the organization you're way more likely to drift into the promotion slow lane.

There are four key players to be aware of:

- Your boss
- Your boss's boss
- Your peers
- HR

Your boss

Make no mistake. Without your boss's firm endorsement and support, a faster-than-usual promotion is not going to happen. Therefore, it is incumbent upon you to stay attuned to what's going on with your boss. Are they a rising star or a sinking ship? What are their strengths? What are their weaknesses?

Understanding what's important to your boss and building this relationship should be an important part of your daily routine.

It's important to realize that most promotions (97 percent) are not decided by hitting a home run in one specific meeting; rather, they are the culmination of one thousand small interactions and "proofs" of your reliability and potential to take on more responsibilities within the team.

This is where all your hard work sending agendas in advance, being organized in your weekly meetings (bullet points), and generally overcommunicating with your boss will pay off. No one else will notice you have been doing all these things every day for the last fifty weeks, but trust me, your boss will notice—and that's your most important audience.

Pro Tip:
Your boss is busy.

One of the most annoying things they have to do is chase down five different team members to gather information for a project or deadline. This represents an opportunity for you to step in and offer to compile everyone's information into a single spreadsheet or email. Yes, it's a little bit of extra work on your part, but your name will start to be associated with delivering the work and you will receive an outsized portion of credit for the total project, thus demonstrating your awesomeness and also showing your boss that you are a leader capable of bringing people and projects together. Boom.

Your boss's boss

It's not just your boss who decides if you get promoted. Your boss's boss, your boss's boss's boss, plus a few higher-level people from other functions and divisions who you've probably never even heard, of are all part of the decision-making process.

This doesn't mean that you need to expend a lot of energy trying to impress the higher-ups or trying to go over your boss's head, but it helps to be aware that there are larger forces at work that all have a say in deciding whether you get promoted. When that time comes, you want everyone to have a positive view of you, regardless of how visible you are to them on a regular basis.

This is where your "network" comes into play. Do you have any mentors? Do you consistently reach out to people beyond your immediate team? Do people in the organization know your name? Being a stranger to everyone but your daily coworkers hinders your ability to get promoted faster than usual.

One easy way to start is by asking people to coffee. This is a low-cost, high-impact solution to meeting new people and letting them get to know who you are. Remember what we talked about on page 32, and focus on making it easy for people to say yes. It is important that this outreach feels organic and authentic, so don't turn this into a death march of forced interactions by trying to meet with every single person in just one or two weeks. People aren't stupid. They'll notice if they are just one of many, so take your time and spread it out.

Getting promoted is a marathon, not a sprint.

Pro Tip:

Get an interesting hobby outside of work.

If you try to build your reputation on good emails and solid business results you might start to blend in with the office furniture and become invisible. Staking a claim to an interesting passion outside of work gives people in the office a reason to engage you in casual conversation. Your goal is simple: you want people to know who you are.

In my case, I always talk about the fact that I am a beekeeper and have 100,000 bees on my roof. Voilà . . . my hero fact. It's amazing how many people will approach me in the hallway and say, "I heard you are a beekeeper. . . ."

Peers

Getting a promotion can be about more than just your own performance. There are a lot of team dynamics that your company will likely have to balance when considering promotions.

Is there a peer who started at the same time as you? If so, this might be a problem because you will be compared with each other—and if they are found lacking, sometimes management won't want to promote one of you without promoting the other. If there's someone who started before you but is in the same position, management may want to avoid promoting a newer hire before a longer-tenured employee.

This exact scenario happened to me when I was up for a promotion at work. My boss actually said, "You are ready Justin—but Carla isn't ready, and we think it will hurt her feelings if you get promoted first." (P.S. Carla went on to a very successful career, so it just goes to show that promotions rarely happen on any exact schedule.)

You need to understand that giving promotions is a very political process.

There may be someone in another division who is also up for a promotion. In this case, your boss has to convince not just their boss, but also their peers that you deserve the promotion—sometimes at the expense of someone else.

The point is, it's bigger than just you and your boss. That is why it is so important that you have built your network and set clear, measurable goals in order to move your promotion from qualitative to quantitative. All of the extra small things you've done along the way (that other people might not have noticed) will pay off at moments like this to tip the scales in your favor. Advantage: you.

HR

Now is a good time to talk about your relationship with HR—or lack thereof—because when you're going for a promotion, HR is inevitably going to be involved.

I can tell you from experience there are good HR people and there are really bad HR people (with little in-between). But no matter where they land on the spectrum of good and bad, you need to have a relationship with them.

I recommend meeting with your HR representative at least four times a year so that you stay familiar; they know what your situation is and what your goals are. You should treat these quarterly meetings as 50 percent "get to know Justin the person" and 50 percent "highlight key accomplishments (business and people)."

Your goal is to move yourself from being just another brick in the wall to a human being, with a family (if applicable), hopes, and dreams. The more that people connect with you on an emotional, human level, the more they will be invested in your success (and promotion).

HR usually has a seat at the table when it comes to the final sign-off for promotions, and if you've cultivated a relationship with HR you are far more likely to get the benefit of the doubt, or perhaps even have an additional advocate for your promotion. So reach out and schedule a meeting today . . .

●　●　●

MAKING YOUR CASE

Approach each promotion as a trial lawyer. Build your case with clear and concise facts, create a believable timeline, and make the jury (your boss and everyone else) feel that it's an easy decision—beyond a reasonable doubt.

There are three steps to making your case for promotion:

- Summarize your accomplishments
- Schedule a meeting
- Meet

Step 1: Summarize your accomplishments

One of the key reasons for writing clear and measurable goals is so that when you accomplish them, no one can dispute your performance. But equally important to setting and achieving your goals is the physical act of summarizing your accomplishments in an effective way. This is about making sure you get credit for everything you have accomplished.

Notice I said that YOU summarize your goals and end-of-year performance. Most people make the mistake of leaving the summary of their accomplishments to their boss. This is the equivalent of running the length of the field and stopping on the one-yard line.

Your boss is busy. Your boss has ninety-nine problems, and your promotion is likely not one of them (meaning they aren't thinking about you as much as you are thinking about you (and your promotion).

You need to do the work so your boss doesn't have to. Write your one-page summary using bullet points, clear headlines, and as few words as possible—while still capturing the quantifiable details.

```
┌─────────────────────── Pro Tip: ───────────────────────┐
│                     Save everything.                     │
│                                                          │
│  Your memory is not as good as you think it is, and      │
│  there's a good chance you won't remember everything     │
│  you accomplished over the course of a full year. What   │
│  happened in February will be a distant memory by        │
│  December—not just for you, but for your boss as well.    │
│  You want to make sure you get full credit for your      │
│  efforts throughout the year so your case for promotion  │
│  is as strong as possible. My easy solution for this     │
│  problem is to create an "accomplishments" folder in     │
│  your email. Save everything. Compliments from your      │
│  boss, project kick-off emails, business results—        │
│  everything counts when it comes to building the case    │
│  for your promotion.                                     │
└──────────────────────────────────────────────────────────┘
```

Step 2: Schedule a meeting

Once you have your bullet-point list of accomplishments, you need to schedule time to review it with your boss.

This is all part of taking control of your own promotion. You do the work so your boss doesn't have to.

Be smart about the timing you set for this meeting.

While the official end-of-year reviews may take place in January, you should be aware that conversations about promotions are likely taking place as early as two months prior to this (end of November or early December). It is essential that you stay ahead of these conversations, because if your boss gets pulled into a meeting to talk about your promotion and they don't have your bullet-point summary sheet, the chances of your promotion just decreased by 50 percent.

If you have trouble finding time on your boss's calendar I recommend that you repurpose one of your weekly 1:1 meetings to talk about your promotion. This is too important to let slip for a few weeks.

Pro Tip:

Send a simple pre-meeting email.

Prior to the actual meeting, you want to give your boss a chance to digest your accomplishments before being confronted in person, so put it all in an email.

Subject: PROMOTION.
Hi Boss, In our 1:1 this week I'd like to spend some time talking about next steps for a potential promotion. To that end, I summarized my key accomplishments over the past 12 months below. Look forward to discussing at our weekly 1:1 meeting on Thursday.

Ideally you should send this email two days prior to the meeting to make sure they have time to read it. The chances of having a constructive conversation during your promotion meeting will increase exponentially if you provide your boss with this summary in advance.

Step 3: Meet

This meeting should be approached as a confirmation rather than a request. You've done the work. Feel confident that your weekly meetings and promotion email have done most of the talking for you, before you even walk into the room. (If you feel there's something new that you need to bring up in this meeting to improve your case, chances are you may have missed a step somewhere along the way.)

Your goal is to set the tone, frame the conversation briefly, and then get out of the way. Explain that the purpose of the meeting is to talk about your prospects for promotion, hand over your bullet-point list of accomplishments, and then shut up and listen. Unlike the rest of your 1:1 meetings, you want to let your boss do the talking.

What happens next totally depends on whether you have an awesome boss, a crappy boss, or a lazy boss.

- **If you have an awesome boss,** they will have already confirmed you are getting a promotion with all the key players—their boss, their boss's boss, HR, and others—in which case, they'll say they don't need you to read each bullet point. They'll tell you everything looks good and they'll take a look at it later. Lucky you.

- **If you have a crappy boss,** they'll sigh heavily and then proceed to tell you why you aren't going to get a promotion. They're not a crappy boss because they didn't promote you—that's your fault. They are a crappy boss because it shouldn't have gotten this far. Getting promoted shouldn't be a surprise ending. It should be a steady and consistent conversation throughout the year, based on the goals you set, the feedback you received, and the constructive conversations along the way.

- **If you have a lazy boss,** they haven't done their homework and haven't laid the foundation with their boss and HR. In this case, they will likely feel a bit of panic and will want to review your list of key accomplishments with you to see if there is enough for them to make a compelling case for your promotion. This isn't an ideal situation, but you can still have confidence because you've done the work, even though your boss hasn't. At this point, the ball is in your boss's hands, but keep the pressure on them by respectfully (and consistently) checking in with them on this topic.

Regardless of what kind of boss you have (good, bad, or lazy), you should feel confident that your weekly meetings and your promotion email have done most of the work before you even walk into the room.

BONUS: KEEP GOING

Whether you get promoted can feel like a make-or-break moment, but the truth is that it doesn't really matter if you get promoted this September or next January. Trust me, it all evens out in the end and, across the entire arc of your career, a few months here or there are not going to make a difference.

Our goal in this chapter is to tip the scales in your favor, so whichever way the wind blows, you can feel good knowing that you did things the right way.

If you get promoted, congratulations. I'm really happy for you, but don't stop now. Sit down with your boss and set new priorities and new goals, and push onward and upward. It's not about the next promotion (don't be greedy) as much as it is about ensuring you are able to meet expectations for your new role. The same rules apply: be specific and stay in constant contact with your boss.

If you don't get promoted, don't give up.

It's important that you learn from the experience and figure out where things went wrong? Is it a you issue? Maybe you overestimated your abilities or misinterpreted feedback? Is it a boss issue? The boss misled you and under-delivered? Is it a company issue? Are they unwilling or unable to promote you because of things beyond your control? Do you need to think about looking for other opportunities? Any combination of these factors can disrupt the best-laid plans for a promotion.

I recommend you schedule some time with HR and ask for some honest feedback about where you are and why you didn't get promoted. You need some perspective from someone slightly less close to the situation to give you a clear picture of where you stand.

Listen carefully, consider your options, and get back to work.

Remember, promotions rarely—if ever—happen at the exact moment that we deserve them, so find solace in Martin Luther King Jr.'s words:

"The arc of the moral universe is long, but it bends toward justice." If you keep working hard and doing the little things right, your (deserved) promotions will happen, and I promise you, at some point in your career, you'll be the one who catches the lucky break to get a promotion earlier than you ever expected.

6.

How to balance life and work

IT'S DOUBTFUL THEY ARE GOING TO LIST THE SPEED OF YOUR PROMOTION OR THE RESULTS OF LAST QUARTER ON YOUR TOMBSTONE.

The people, the laughs, the skills you learn—those are the things you'll take with you for the rest of your life.

It's easy to get caught up in the day-to-day drama of the workplace. (He doesn't like her, she doesn't like anyone, and round and round it goes.) It's important that you keep perspective on what matters and what doesn't, because if you aren't careful, work can become all-consuming.

It is not uncommon to see people forego their planned vacation (or work an extra three hours into the night) because they have to work on a project. The truth is, that project would get done with or without you—or, just as likely, the deadline is arbitrary and you can ask for an extension if you plan in advance.

This isn't to say that none of the work you do matters. It can and often does. My point is simply to highlight the trap that people fall into at work: prioritizing a project over their personal life, and in so doing, convincing themselves that they couldn't possibly take time for themselves.

As such, work-life balance is often treated like the holy grail—rumored but never found. Well, I for one wholly and completely reject this idea. In fact,

I posit that work-life balance can be easily achieved—if you want it badly enough to actually put some effort into achieving it.

To start, be good at your job. Get sh*t done and avoid office politics, because it's a waste of your time and energy. Second, decide what is most important to you (family, gym, travel, friends), and then build your day toward achieving it. It's that simple. Decide what you want, and then organize yourself to get it.

During my years climbing the ladder of corporate America I've written fourteen books, toured the country in a rock band, started a record label, taken twenty-eight-day vacations, and installed 100,000 bees on my roof. I made it a personal rule to never check email after 5 p.m. and never do a single minute of work on a weekend.

I say all this because I hope you realize that the tips and tricks that we've talked about in this book— writing good emails, sending agendas in advance, using bullet points, setting specific deadlines—aren't just dumb work stuff to make your job go better. They are actually the secrets to being good at your job so you can get on with your life and do more of the things you love.

HOW TO CREATE "ME" TIME (DURING THE WORKWEEK)

It's important to realize that work-life balance doesn't only exist outside the office. There are a lot of small things you can do during your workday to ensure that you are staying connected to the rest of the world and keeping yourself fresh and energized by the people and places around you.

Here are three easy ways to carve out "me" time in your otherwise over-programmed workweek.

Get to work early

Yes, we've already talked about the benefits of getting to work early as it relates to your performance on the job, but I want to quickly highlight the benefits for your work-life balance.

Every fifteen minutes you spend at your desk before everyone else arrives is worth thirty minutes toward an earlier departure at the end of the day. This means that if you can get to work thirty minutes early in the morning, you will be able to leave work one hour earlier. Thus, one hour earlier in the morning translates to being home two hours earlier in the evening. Don't believe me? Try it.

Now, what you choose to do with those two hours is up to you. Play with the kids, drink with friends, get to the gym . . . the point is, your life is the choices you make, so decide if one extra snooze button is worth staying at the office for an extra thirty minutes.

Pro Tip:

Make mornings work time and evenings play time.

In all my years of working in corporate America, I've never had anyone invite me to hang out and do something fun at 7 a.m.

I have, however, had plenty of fun invitations and opportunities present themselves at 6 p.m. Having to say no to those things because you have "more work to do" builds resentment toward your job and causes you to miss out on life.

Eat lunch outside

It is important that you keep yourself fresh during the day (and the week). Stepping outside for a walk at lunch is a no-cost investment in your mental and physical health.

Leave your phone at your desk and just walk. It's a great chance to remind yourself that there is an entire world out there, and taking thirty minutes outside for lunch can provide much-needed perspective, especially when things at work are "hard" or "overwhelming." It is at these times, more than ever, that you need to invest in yourself and give yourself a little break.

The timing may not work out every single day, but overall, you should be making time to step outside at least four days per week. Whether it's an afternoon coffee break, a fast lunch in the cafeteria paired with a meandering walk around the block, or stepping outside to call an old friend for ten minutes before heading back up to your desk, it is important to prioritize getting out of the office building on a regular basis.

The point is to give yourself a break from the office routine (this report in this basket on this day at this time . . .) and keep your mind and body fresh.

So shake things up. Do something different today. Walk three blocks in a direction you've never been. A likely side effect is that you'll find new ideas inspired by new inputs, so even your work will benefit from your non-work efforts.

Pro Tip:

Make a habit of grabbing random coworkers for these pop-out sessions.

Especially on the coffee breaks in the afternoon, these brief ten-minute walks can build your network and keep the human connection alive in the workplace.

Take a class

It is important to be attuned to the moments at work when things feel a little bit easier—or less busy. Rather than settling for being bored, I would encourage you to find stimulation from projects outside work.

There will be plenty of days and weeks (and months) when work is really, really hard, so take advantage of the moments when it eases up, and do something purposeful.

Sign up for a random class during the workweek. No matter where you live, there are countless classes for drawing, painting, ceramics, beekeeping, or anything your heart desires.

I recommend that you make your boss feel like a part of the journey. Ask their permission; explain that you want to try something new and mention that it will require you to leave by 5:30 on Wednesdays. Voilà—you have given yourself a wonderful excuse to leave work early, you'll learn something new, AND your boss will be flattered to think they are contributing to this opportunity. Everybody wins.

HOW TO LEAVE WORK AT WORK

Leaving work at work is easier said than done. It requires systems of both physical and mental separation to completely disconnect your personal life from your work life and create more room for the more important things—friends, family, and social media.

Put your phone away

The most dangerous instrument for undermining your work-life balance is your phone. It is the Trojan horse of work-life balance. Know your enemy.

Here are my three simple rules to avoid letting work seep into your personal life:

- **Hear no evil:** When you leave work turn your work phone to silent.

- **See no evil (part 1):** When you get home, put your work phone somewhere that is out of sight, in order to keep it out of mind. (I usually hide my phone in a drawer when I get home.)

- **See no evil (part 2):** If you have to have your work email on your personal phone, do not leave your work email app on the home screen of your phone. Seeing a notification that shows new emails will only serve to stress and distract you while you are outside the office.

Don't bring your work home

If you don't finish a project by end of day, I recommend you leave it at work and come in early the next day to finish it. This is all about establishing a physical barrier between work and the rest of your life.

Bringing work home with you (whether your computer or actual papers) can have a corrosive effect on your work-life balance.

Nine times out of ten you won't do the work anyway, so don't (literally) burden yourself with having to physically carry work home with you.

Lighten your load, and remind yourself that keeping a strong separation of church and state is important to maintaining balance in democracies, so you should take the same care in achieving balance in your work and personal life.

Don't worry

Nothing important happens between 7 p.m. and 7 a.m. during the work-week, and the same is definitely true about the weekends.

It is important that you internalize and believe this to be true if you are going to be successful at mentally letting go of work when you leave the office.

In my experience, there are always a few people who revel in sending emails back and forth over the weekend, but ten times out of ten nothing is ever decided (or changed), so skip all the drama and enjoy your time off.

HOW TO TAKE
TIME OFF

Taking time off from work is critical to your ability to be good at your job. If you can't unplug, refresh, and let go, you are much more likely to get burned out or run out of new ideas, so give yourself a break and invest some time and energy into figuring out how to get away.

Volunteer

Not to be cynical, but the best thing about volunteering is that you can do it during work hours and everyone will love you for it. Find a charity in your city that you believe in, and sign up to do something once per month during normal work hours.

Chances are, your company already has a relationship with an existing charity, so all you have to do is reach out to them and figure out all the ways (and times) that you and your coworkers could volunteer during a normal workweek.

Boom—now you get a two-hour break once a month to get out of the office and find perspective, happiness, and the satisfaction of giving your time to a good cause. (Not to mention that you look like a selfless leader who organizes the team for special projects.)

Nice work.

Take vacations

Vacation. Vacation. Vacation. Everybody loves it, but most people suck at doing it.

Here are the four steps to being good at taking vacation:

- **Asking for vacation:** The key is to work far in advance. There is a direct correlation between how far in advance you request a vacation and your likelihood of getting approval. This same equation is applicable for the length of your vacation, meaning that three-week "sabbatical" isn't out of reach if you can plan far enough in advance and make it easy for your boss to say yes. (See page 32 for details.)

- **Prepping for vacation:** In the days and weeks leading up to your vacation it is important that you create and maintain as much visibility as possible for your impending break. This isn't about bragging; this is about ensuring that everyone knows what is going on and people are prepared to cover for you. Done correctly, this is an opportunity to demonstrate how organized you are by ensuring that all your work is delivered at least twenty-four hours prior to your departure, rather than half-completed as you walk out the door. Don't overlook these small moments that can make or break your reputation as someone who is reliable and takes care of business.

- **Talking about vacation:** Most people miss this, but talking about your vacation (before and after) is a great opportunity to build your personal brand. If you are going on vacation with your extended family, be sure to romance the old family cabin as a reflection of your family-first approach (i.e., I'm a good person). If you are going to Ibiza to dance your ass off, talk about visiting Greece and going somewhere new, rather than how drunk you are going to get. People are going to ask, so do yourself a favor and have a good story and a good hero fact. (See page 80.)

- **Taking vacation:** When it comes to the actual taking of vacation, enjoy yourself. Don't think about work, certainly don't do work, and if you tend to feel guilty about either of those recommendations, remind yourself that you give that company (at least) 261 workdays per year, so it is not too much to take less than 10 percent (twenty-one days or fewer) for yourself.

About the Author

Author of the rogue corporate playbook HOW TO BE A BOSS and mouthpiece of MR CORPO podcast, Justin is a self-described efficiency monster. He has been the youngest senior executive at some of the world's biggest apparel companies including Gap, Old Navy, Levi's, and UNIQLO, running billion-dollar businesses while finding time to write fourteen books, tour the country in a rock band, and keep 100,000 bees on his roof. Justin is currently president of Imprint Projects in New York City. Best to follow him on Instagram @mrcorpo or www.mrcorpo.com.